Daily Prayers to Saint Joseph

from the 1910 Raccolta

Shalone Cason

Public Domain text From the 1910 Raccolta by Ambrose St. John
IMPRIMATUR: EDMUNDUS SURMONT, Vicarius Generalis. 1909

Cover and interior design by: Shalone Cason

Contents

Sunday

PURE spouse of most holy Mary, glorious St Joseph, the trouble and anguish of thy heart were great when, being in sore perplexity, thou wast minded to put away thy stainless spouse; yet was thy joy inexpressible when the Archangel revealed to thee the sublime mystery of the Incarnation. By this thy sorrow and thy joy, we pray thee comfort our souls now and in their last pains with the consolation of a well-spent life, and a holy death like unto thy own, with JESUS and Mary at our side.

PATER, Ave, Gloria.

V/. Pray for us, holy Joseph.
R/. That we may be made worthy of the promises of CHRIST.

Let us pray.

O GOD, who in thine ineffable providence didst vouchsafe to choose blessed Joseph to be the spouse of thy most holy Mother; grant, we beseech Thee, that we may have him for our intercessor in heaven, whom on earth we venerate as our holy Protector. Who livest and reignest, world without end. Amen.

Monday

MOST blessed Patriarch, glorious St Joseph, chosen to the office of Father of the Word made Man, the pain was keen that thou didst feel when thou didst see the Infant JESUS born in abject poverty; but thy pain was changed into heavenly joy when thou didst hear the harmony of angel-choirs, and behold the glory of that night. By this thy sorrow and thy joy, we pray thee obtain for us that, when the journey of our life is ended, we too may pass to that blessed land where we shall hear the angel-chants, and rejoice in the bright light of heavenly glory.

PATER, Ave, Gloria.

V/. Pray for us, holy Joseph.
R/. That we may be made worthy of the promises of CHRIST.

Let us pray.

O GOD, who in thine ineffable providence didst vouchsafe to choose blessed Joseph to be the spouse of thy most holy Mother; grant, we beseech Thee, that we may have him for our intercessor in heaven, whom on earth we venerate as our holy Protector. Who livest and reignest, world without end. Amen.

Tuesday

O THOU who wast ever most obedient in executing the law of GOD, glorious St Joseph, thy heart was pierced with pain when the precious Blood of the Infant SAVIOUR was shed at his Circumcision; but with the Name of JESUS new life and heavenly joy returned to thee. By this thy sorrow and thy joy, obtain for us that, being freed, while we still live, from every vice, we too may cheerfully die with the sweet Name of JESUS in our hearts and on our lips.

PATER, Ave, Gloria.

V/. Pray for us, holy Joseph.
R/. That we may be made worthy of the promises of CHRIST.

Let us pray.

O GOD, who in thine ineffable providence didst vouchsafe to choose blessed Joseph to be the spouse of thy most holy Mother; grant, we beseech Thee, that we may have him for our intercessor in heaven, whom on earth we venerate as our holy Protector. Who livest and reignest, world without end. Amen.

Wednesday

MOST faithful Saint, glorious St Joseph, who wast admitted to take part in the redemption of man; the prophecy of Simeon foretelling the sufferings of JESUS and Mary caused thee a pang like that of death, but, at the same time, by his prediction of the salvation and glorious resurrection of innumerable souls, filled thee with great joy. By this thy sorrow and thy joy, help us with thy prayers to be of the number of those who, by the merits of JESUS and the intercession of his Virgin Mother, shall be partakers of the resurrection to glory.

PATER, Ave, Gloria.

V/. Pray for us, holy Joseph.
R/. That we may be made worthy of the promises of CHRIST.

Let us pray.

O GOD, who in thine ineffable providence didst vouchsafe to choose blessed Joseph to be the spouse of thy most holy Mother; grant, we beseech Thee, that we may have him for our intercessor in heaven, whom on earth we venerate as our holy Protector. Who livest and reignest, world without end. Amen.

Thursday

MOST watchful Guardian, glorious St Joseph, who wast so intimately familiar with the Incarnate SON of GOD, greatly thou didst toil to nurture and to serve the SON of the Most High, especially in the flight thou madest with Him into Egypt; greatly also didst thou rejoice to have GOD Himself always with thee, and to see the overthrow of the idols of Egypt. By this thy sorrow and thy joy, obtain for us grace to keep far out of the reach of the enemy of our souls, by quitting all dangerous occasions, that so no idol of earthly affection may any longer occupy a place in our hearts, but that, being entirely devoted to the service of JESUS and Mary, we may live and die for them alone.

PATER, Ave, Gloria.

V/. Pray for us, holy Joseph.

R/. That we may be made worthy of the promises of CHRIST.

Let us pray.

O GOD, who in thine ineffable providence didst vouchsafe to choose blessed Joseph to be the spouse of thy most holy Mother; grant, we beseech Thee, that we may have him for our intercessor in heaven, whom on earth we venerate as our holy Protector. Who livest and reignest, world without end. Amen.

Friday

ANGEL on earth, glorious St Joseph, who didst so wonder to see the King of Heaven obedient to thy bidding, the consolation thou hadst at his return from Egypt was disturbed by the fear of Archelaus, but nevertheless, being reassured by the angel, thou didst go back and dwell happily at Nazareth, in the company of JESUS and Mary. By this thy sorrow and thy joy, obtain for us that, having our hearts freed from idle fears, we may enjoy the peace of a tranquil conscience, dwelling safely with JESUS and Mary, and dying at last in their arms.

PATER, Ave, Gloria.

V/. Pray for us, holy Joseph.
R/. That we may be made worthy of the promises of CHRIST.

Let us pray.

O GOD, who in thine ineffable providence didst vouchsafe to choose blessed Joseph to be the spouse of thy most holy Mother; grant, we beseech Thee, that we may have him for our intercessor in heaven, whom on earth we venerate as our holy Protector. Who livest and reignest, world without end. Amen.

Saturday

EXAMPLE of holy living, glorious St Joseph, when through no fault of thine thou didst lose JESUS, the Holy Child, thou didst search for Him with great sorrow for three days, until with joy unspeakable thou didst find Him, who was thy Life, amidst the doctors in the Temple. By this thy sorrow and thy joy, we pray thee with our whole hearts so to interpose always in our behalf, that we may never lose JESUS by mortal sin, and if we are at any time so wretched as to lose Him, then we pray thee to aid us to seek Him with unwearied sorrow until we find Him, particularly in the hour of our death, that we may pass from this life to enjoy Him for ever in heaven, there to sing with thee his divine mercies without end.

PATER, Ave, Gloria.

V/. Pray for us, holy Joseph.

R/. That we may be made worthy of the promises of CHRIST.

Let us pray.

O GOD, who in thine ineffable providence didst vouchsafe to choose blessed Joseph to be the spouse of thy most holy Mother; grant, we beseech Thee, that we may have him for our intercessor in heaven, whom on earth we venerate as our holy Protector. Who livest and reignest, world without end. Amen.

St. Joseph's Responsory

TO all who would holily live,
To all who would happily die
St Joseph is ready to give,
Sure guidance, and help from on high.

Of Mary the spouse undefil'd,
Just, holy, and pure of all stain,
He asks of his own foster Child,
And needs but ask to obtain.

To all who would holily live,
To all who would happily die
St Joseph is ready to give,
Sure guidance, and help from on high.

In the manger that Child he adored

And nursed Him in exile and flight;
Him, lost in his boyhood, deplored,
And found with amaze and delight.

To all who would holily live,
To all who would happily die
St Joseph is ready to give,
Sure guidance, and help from on high.

The Maker of heaven and earth
By the labour of Joseph was fed;
The SON by an infinite birth
Submissive to Joseph was made.

To all who would holily live,
To all who would happily die
St Joseph is ready to give,
Sure guidance, and help from on high.

And when his last hour drew nigh,
Oh, full of all joy was his breast,
Seeing JESUS and Mary close by,
As he tranquilly slumbered to rest.

To all who would holily live,
To all who would happily die
St Joseph is ready to give,
Sure guidance, and help from on high.

All praise to the FATHER above;
All praise to his glorious SON;
All praise to the SPIRIT of love,
While the days of eternity run.

Ant. Behold the faithful and prudent servant whom the
LORD set over his house.

V/. Pray for us, holy Joseph.

R/. That we may be made worthy of the promises of CHRIST.

Let us pray.

O GOD, who in thy ineffable providence didst vouchsafe to choose blessed Joseph to be the spouse of thy most holy Mother, grant, we beseech Thee, that we may have him for our intercessor in Heaven, whom on earth we venerate as our most holy protector. Who livest and reignest, etc. Amen.

Prayer to St Joseph, Patron of the Universal Church

O MOST powerful Patriarch, St Joseph, Patron of that universal Church which has always invoked thee in anxieties and tribulations; from the lofty seat of thy glory lovingly regard the Catholic world. Let it move thy paternal heart to see the mystical Spouse of CHRIST and his Vicar weakened by sorrow and persecuted by powerful enemies. We beseech thee, by the most bitter suffering thou didst experience on earth, to wipe away in mercy the tears of the revered Pontiff, to defend and liberate him, and to intercede with the Giver of peace and charity, that every hostile power being overcome and every error being destroyed, the whole Church may serve the GOD of all blessings in perfect liberty: ut destructis adversitatibus et erroribus universis Ecclesiæ secura DEO serviat libertate. Amen.

O GLORIOUS St Joseph, chosen by GOD to be the reputed father of JESUS, the most pure spouse of Mary ever Virgin, and the head of the Holy Family, and then elected by the Vicar of CHRIST to be the heavenly Patron and Protector of the Church founded by JESUS CHRIST; with the greatest confidence I implore at this time thy powerful aid for the entire Church militant. Protect in a special manner with thy truly paternal love the Supreme Pontiff and all the bishops and priests united to the See of St Peter. Defend all those who labour for souls in the midst of the afflictions and tribulations of this life, and obtain the willing submission of every nation throughout the world to the Church, the necessary means of salvation for all.

O dearest St Joseph, be pleased to accept the consecration which I make to thee of myself. I dedicate myself entirely to thee that thou mayest ever be my father, my protector, and my guide in the way of salvation. Obtain for me great purity of heart and a fervent love of the interior life. Grant that after thy example all my actions may be directed to the greater glory of GOD, in union with the divine Heart of JESUS and the immaculate heart of Mary, and with thee. Finally, pray for me that I may be able to share in the peace and joy of thy most holy death. Amen.

Prayers for those in their Agony

ETERNAL FATHER, by the love which Thou bearest to St Joseph, chosen by Thee from among all men to represent Thee on earth, have pity on us and on poor souls in their agony. PATER, Ave, Gloria. Eternal and divine SON, by the love which Thou bearest to St Joseph, thy most faithful guardian on earth, have pity on us and on all poor souls in their agony. PATER, Ave, Gloria. Eternal and divine SPIRIT, by the love Thou bearest to St Joseph, who with so great solicitude watched over most holy Mary the Spouse of thy predilection, have pity on us and on all poor souls in their agony. PATER, Ave, Gloria.

TO thee, O blessed Joseph, do we fly in our tribulation, and having implored the help of thy most holy spouse, we confidently crave thy patronage also. Through that charity which bound thee to the Immaculate Virgin Mother of GOD, and through the paternal love with which thou didst embrace the Child JESUS, we humbly beseech thee graciously to regard the inheritance which JESUS CHRIST hath purchased by his Blood, and with thy power and strength to aid us in our necessities. O most watchful Guardian of the Divine Family, defend the chosen children of JESUS CHRIST; O most loving Father, ward off from us every contagion of error and corrupting influence; O our most mighty protector, be propitious to us and from Heaven assist us in this our struggle with the power of darkness; and, as once thou didst rescue the Child JESUS from deadly peril, so now protect GOD'S holy Church from the snares of the enemy and from all adversity: shield, too, each one of us by thy constant protection, so that, supported by thine example and thine aid, we may be able to live piously, to die holily, and to obtain eternal happiness in Heaven. Amen

Short Prayers to St. Joseph

O JOSEPH, virgo pater JESU, purissime sponse Virginis Mariæ, quotidie deprecare pro nobis ipsum JESUM FILIUM DEI, ut, armis suæ gratiæ muniti, legitime certantes in vita ab eodem coronemur in morte.

O JOSEPH, virgin father of JESUS, most pure spouse of the Virgin Mary, pray for us daily to the SON of GOD, that, armed with the weapons of his grace, we may fight as we ought in life, and be crowned by Him in death.

GLORIOUS St Joseph, model of all those who are devoted to labour, obtain for me the grace to work in a spirit of penance for the expiation of my many sins; to work conscientiously, putting the call of duty above my inclinations; to work with gratitude and joy, considering it an honour to employ and develop, by means of labour, the gifts received from GOD; to work with order, peace, moderation and patience, without ever recoiling before weariness or difficulties; to work, above all, with purity of intention, and with detachment from self, having always death before my eyes and the account which I must render of time lost, of talents wasted, of good omitted, of vain complacency in success, so fatal to the work of GOD. All for JESUS, all for Mary, all after thy example, O Patriarch Joseph. Such shall be my watchword in life and in death. Amen.

REMEMBER, most pure spouse of Mary ever Virgin, my loving protector, St Joseph, that never has it been heard that anyone ever invoked thy protection, or besought aid of thee, without being consoled. In this confidence I come before thee, I fervently recommend myself to thee. Despise not my prayer, foster-father of our REDEEMER, but do thou in thy pity receive it. Amen.

VIRGINUM custos, et pater Sancte Joseph, cujus fideli custodiæ ipsa innocentia CHRISTUS JESUS, et Virgo virginum, Maria commissa fuit; te per hoc utrumque carissimum pignus, JESUM et Mariam, obsecro, et obtestor, ut me ab omni immunditia præservatum, mente incontaminata, puro corde et casto corpore JESU et Mariæ semper facias castissime famulari. Amen.

GUARDIAN of virgins, and holy father Joseph, to whose faithful custody CHRIST JESUS Innocence itself, and Mary, Virgin of virgins, were committed; I pray and beseech thee, by these dear pledges, JESUS and Mary, that, being preserved from all uncleanness, I may with spotless mind, pure heart and chaste body, ever serve JESUS and Mary most chastely all the days of my life. Amen.

Afterword

Please go to casoncatholic.com/books to find more prayer books from Shalone Cason.
Thank you and God bless +

Also, please leave a review on Amazon.

Printed in Great Britain
by Amazon

35872094R00020